"I guess we're going to ......,
Brother.

They kissed.

Brother blushed.

They kissed again.

Brother blushed again.

They kissed again and again and
again...

The Berenstain Bears and the NEW GIRL IN TOWN

by Stan & Jan Berenstain

A BIG CHAPTER BOOK™

Random House New York

Library of Congress Cataloging-in-Publication Data
Berenstain, Stan.
The Berenstain Bears and the new girl in town /
by Stan & Jan Berenstain.
        p. cm. — (A Big chapter book)
SUMMARY: Brother Bear's budding romance with Squire Grizzly's niece helps bring about an end to the fierce feud between the Grizzly and Bear clans.
ISBN 0-679-83613-6 (pbk.) — ISBN 0-679-93613-0 (lib. bdg.)
[1. Prejudices—Fiction. 2. Friendship—Fiction. 3. Bears—Fiction.] I. Berenstain, Jan. II. Title. III. Series: Berenstain, Stan. Big chapter book.
PZ7.B4483Bejo 1993
[Fic.]—dc20   92-32570

Manufactured in the United States of America 10 9 8 7 6 5

BIG CHAPTER BOOKS is a trademark of Berenstain Enterprises, Inc.

Contents

Chapter 1
Something in the Air

There was no question about it. A new season had come to Bear Country. Its signs were everywhere as Brother Bear, Sister Bear, and Cousin Freddy walked home from school. Flowers covered the lawns. Trees were in bloom. Birds were building their nests. And many of the boy and girl cubs were walking along in pairs. Some of them were even holding hands! Yes, spring had sprung in Bear Country. Romance was in the air!

"Romance," said Brother Bear. He looked at two older cubs holding hands and made a face. "Disgusting."

"Sickening," said Cousin Freddy.

Sister looked up at the boys and rolled her eyes. She thought romance was great! Just to bug her brother and cousin, she started singing a well-known song:

"Beeswax!" said Brother.

"You don't understand," teased Sister. "It's love that makes the world go round."

"Double beeswax!" Brother shouted.

Freddy, who liked reading the encyclopedia for fun, also disagreed with Sister. "What makes the world go around," he said, "is the inertial effect on our solar system of the energy generated by the Big Bang. At least, that's the latest theory."

"What I get a big bang out of," said Sister, "is you two. You're scared of girls! Why don't you take it easy and go with the flow?"

"I'm *not* scared of girls!" said Brother. "Some of my best friends are girls."

Just then they heard a girl's voice calling out, "Brother, oh, *Bro-ther!* Wait up."

"I think it's one of your best friends," said Sister.

Brother turned and saw Babs Bruno and some other girls from his class. They were hurrying to catch up with him. Babs's friends were giggling.

"Hi, Babs," said Brother.

Babs looked up at him. She smiled sweetly. "I could use some help with tonight's math homework," she purred. "Could you come over?"

Brother started to blush, "I—uh—I'll call you . . ." Heat was creeping up from under his collar. "Maybe we can do it by phone," he said. Brother felt his ears catch fire. He knew what that meant. He was blushing like crazy.

"I'll be *wait-ing*," sang Babs. Then she and her giggling friends ran off.

"Don't say a word!" Brother warned Sister.

Sister opened her mouth and took hold of the tip of her tongue.

"What in the world are you doing?" said Freddy.

"Holding my tongue," mumbled Sister. Then she let go and laughed. "Really, Brother, everyone knows Babs Bruno has a major crush on you. Why not give her a break?"

"Why don't you give *me* a break?" said Brother. "Look, I like Babs. She's nice. But I just don't go for all this cub romance stuff. It's phony baloney. It's just a bunch of silly cubs trying to act grown up."

"For example," said Freddy. He pointed ahead.

"Well, well," said Sister. "Looks like the on-again, off-again thing between Too-Tall Grizzly and Queenie McBear is on again."

Freddy shook his head. "Just look at them."

"No, thanks," said Brother.

It looked as if the Too-Tall and Queenie thing was *really* on again. They weren't just holding hands. They were hanging all over each other.

Suddenly a strange and disturbing thing happened. A truck pulled to a stop next to Queenie and Too-Tall. Two-Ton Grizzly, Too-Tall's dad, climbed out. He grabbed Too-Tall and pulled him into the truck. Then he drove quickly away. Brother, Sister, and Freddy ran over to Queenie.

"What was *that* all about?" asked Brother.

"I d-don't know!" said Queenie.

"Did Two-Ton say anything?" Sister asked.

"Yes . . . but it didn't make any sense."

"What did he say?" Freddy asked.

"He said . . . he said it wasn't right for a member of the Grizzly clan to be seen with a member of the Bear clan."

The cubs looked at one another. Queenie was right. It didn't make sense. It seemed that romance wasn't the only thing in the air. There was something else. Something strange. And it didn't feel good—it didn't feel good at all.

Chapter 2
An Ancient Feud

"Babs isn't the *only* girl with a crush on Brother, you know," Sister said to Mama and Papa. Mama was sewing and Papa was resting in his easy chair, while Brother lay on the floor reading a book. "Why, there's Annie O'Bear, Christine Grizzly, Susie Ursavitch . . ."

Brother gave Sister an angry look and went back to his book.

"Getting to be quite the ladies' man, eh?" teased Papa with a chuckle. "Must take after your old man. Why, in my day—"

"Oh, sure," said Mama. "Before your papa and I were married, he was so shy that

I almost had to ask HIM to get married. Really, the two of you should go easy on Brother. He doesn't have to rush into this boy-girl business if he doesn't want to."

Just then the phone rang. Sister jumped up to answer it. Her eyes lit up when she heard who it was. She gave Brother a teasing *you-know-who* look. "It's for you, loverboy," she said. Then she giggled and handed Brother the phone.

"Hello? Oh, hi, Babs," Brother said. He blushed hot pink. "Oh, yeah, the homework. Right. Just a minute."

Brother grabbed his homework and returned to the phone. "Number one . . . let's see . . . the answer is forty-two. Yeah, you use length times width—that's the formula for the area of a rectangle. Do I know the formula for WHAT? For a HEART?"

Brother's blush turned deep red. Sister squealed into the sofa cushions. "No, I don't want to come over and work on it, Babs," said Brother. "You're more into that kind of—uh—formula than I am . . . Gee, it's getting kind of late, Babs—good night." He hung up and gave Sister Bear an angry look.

"One of your fans?" asked Papa on his way to the kitchen.

"Now, Papa," said Mama. But before she could get another word out, a loud "Phooey!" rang out from the kitchen.

"Onions!" yelled Papa. He pointed to the glass of milk in his hand. "Tastes like onions! Ugh!"

Sister took the glass from Papa and sniffed. "It even SMELLS like onions!"

Mama was trying to clean up the milk Papa had gotten on his overalls when he spat out the bad-tasting stuff. "Now, what do you think happened to make the milk—" she started to say.

"I don't HAVE to think," said Papa. "It has to do with the clover meadow between Farmer Ben's farm and Squire Grizzly's estate. I heard all about it at Zeb's Hardware today."

"The clover meadow?" said Mama. "That's where Ben grazes his cows in the spring to keep them away from the onion grass."

"That's just it. Squire Grizzly fenced it

off. He says it's Grizzly land—always has been. And he says Farmer Ben has no right to use it. He says no member of the Bear clan has any right to it." Papa made a face. "I like onions," he said, "and I like milk. But I do not like ONION MILK! Ugh!"

"I'll make you some tea to get the taste out of your mouth," Mama said. "But I'll tell you something. I don't like all this 'Grizzly land, Bear clan' talk. It sounds like feud talk to me. And modern-day Bear Country doesn't need to have that old feud started up again."

"Feud?" said Brother. "What feud?"

"What *is* a feud?" asked Sister.

"Well," said Papa, "a feud is a fight. But it's a special kind of fight. It's usually between families. And most of the time it goes on for years and years. Sometimes it goes way, way back—like this one. It started when Bear Country was first settled. There was trouble between members of those first families. Then, over the years, the trouble built up into a feud."

"We're members of the Bear family, aren't we, Dad?" asked Brother.

"That's right, Son," said Papa. "You and Sister are . . . let's see, now. You are the great-great-great-grandcubs of old Ebenezer Bear, who was the head of the Bear family."

"Who was the other family?" asked Sister.

"Why, the Grizzly family, of course—headed by old Abner Grizzly."

"What did they fight about?" asked Sister.

"You name it, they fought about it," said Papa. "They fought over boundaries, pasture land, and water rights. Why, they even fought about what to name the place."

"Our family must have won that one, because we're called Bear Country," said Brother.

"That's right, Son." Papa pointed toward the window. "But those mountains over there are the Great Grizzly Mountains. And we've got Lake Grizzly and the Great Grizzly Forest, too."

"So I guess the two families learned to get along," said Sister.

"Oh, after some time. New families moved in, Grizzlys and Bears married, and so on. But things were pretty hot and heavy for a while in the beginning."

"What started the feud?" Brother asked.

"I'm glad you asked that question, Son," said Papa. "What started the whole thing was . . . um, let's see . . . er, way back in the beginning . . ." Papa frowned. "Mama, do you remember what started it?"

"Listen to you," said Mama. "The truth is, cubs, *no one*—no member of either clan—remembers what started it. And if anything shows how silly the whole thing is, *that* does."

"Now wait just a minute," said Papa. He puffed his chest out. "I'll admit that the idea of a war between two clans seems old-fashioned now. But things were different then. Those were special times. Everyone had to protect what they had. And there were heroes on both sides. We had old Ulysses S. Bear on our side. And there was Stonewall Grizzly on the other." Papa was getting all excited as he went on. "You have to admire their courage. Each clan protected its own. Each clan stood up for itself."

"Arguing, fighting, calling names, being mean and nasty," said Mama. "Special times, indeed!"

Papa grinned. He looked a little ashamed. "The truth is, your mama's right," he said. "It *was* silly. But don't worry. No one is going to start it all up again. We're all civilized now. We can settle our little arguments and differences without fighting."

"Fencing off the clover meadow and ruining Farmer Ben's milk doesn't sound very civilized to me. It could lead to a fight," said Brother. He was happy that the family was finally talking about something besides his trouble with girls.

"You're right, of course," said Papa. "What I heard at Zeb's was probably just gossip. Ben's a sensible guy. He wouldn't let some feud from hundreds of years ago start

up again. And if there's any Grizzly we Bears get along with, it's the Squire."

"That's right," said Mama. "Just look at all the work Papa's done for him over the years."

"I've made all that furniture for his mansion," said Papa proudly. "Why, there are tons of antiques out in the shed he wants me to refinish. As a matter of fact," he added, "I should be calling him with a price for the job right now. Maybe I can find out how true this gossip is." But as he was about to pick up the phone, it rang.

"Hello?" answered Papa. "Squire! My goodness! I was just about to call you. What I had in mind was—" But Papa never got to say what it was. He never had a chance.

The Squire started shouting and didn't stop. Mama and the cubs couldn't hear *what* he was saying. But they could hear the angry sound of his voice clear across the room.

Papa could hear what the Squire was saying, though. And he didn't like it one bit. At first, Papa was so surprised he couldn't speak. But by the time his voice came back, he was so angry he was shouting just as loudly as the Squire.

"Oh, yeah?" shouted Papa. "Well, that goes double for you and all the members of the Grizzly clan! . . . you . . . you . . . you MILK POISONER!"

The Squire's shouting ended with a crash. Papa stared at the phone. "He . . . he . . . he hung up on me!"

CLICK!

It was Mama's turn to be angry. "It's no wonder, the way you spoke to him," she said. "You didn't even find out why he called in the first place."

"Oh, yes, I did," Papa said.

"Well? What did he say?" said Mama.

Papa looked even more angry now.

"He said to forget about all the work I was going to do for him!"

"Oh, dear!" said Mama.

"He said that meadow has been Grizzly land for hundreds of years. He called Ben a 'clover thief'! Then he said there was no way

a member of the great Grizzly clan could do business with any member of the lowlife Bear clan. Just like a Grizzly, that no-good snob!"

Mama sighed. "Oh, dear. The feud is back. And it's starting to spread."

"Mama," said Brother, "I'm afraid the feud has already spread further than you think." He told his parents about what had happened to Too-Tall on the way home from school.

Mama put her hand to her mouth. "Dear me, Two-Ton really grabbed him like that and said those things? This is worse than I thought. What's next?"

"*I'll* tell you what's next," Papa shouted. "From now on, none of us Bears will buy anything at any Grizzly-owned store! We won't give the Grizzlys ANY business!"

"But, Papa," Mama said, "Squire Grizzly owns half of Bear Country! Why, there's the big Grizzly gas-station chain, the Grizzly Department Store, and all the Grizzburger fast-food restaurants. And we'll have to take all our savings out of the Great Grizzly National Bank—"

"First thing tomorrow morning!" shouted Papa. He put on his hat and stomped out the door.

"Where are you going?" asked Sister.

"To tell all the Bears to stop buying Grizzly goods!" Papa yelled back.

The next thing Mama and the cubs heard was Papa's car starting up. It sputtered to life and roared down the road before fading away into the night.

"Gosh," said Brother, "I've never seen Papa so angry. May I wait up for him to find out what happens?"

Mama shook her head. "I don't think Papa will be in any mood to talk after all that walking."

"Walking?" said Sister. "He took the car."

"I know," said Mama. She sounded tired. "But the gas tank is almost empty. And the only gas stations within miles of here belong to Squire You-Know-Who."

Chapter 3
New Girl

The next morning, Papa sat grumbling at the kitchen table. He was soaking his sore feet in a bucket of hot water.

"Called Farmer Ben to bring me a can of gas. Had to walk six miles to a phone. But it was worth it. No way was I going to buy gas from a Grizzly. No way! . . . Yikes! Ouch! Not so hot!" Papa begged as Mama added

more water to his footbath.

Brother looked at Sister and pointed to the side of his head. He made a circling motion. Which wasn't very nice, but he really felt that Squire Grizzly, Farmer Ben, Too-Tall's dad, *and* Papa were acting . . . well, a little nutty.

Sister nodded in agreement. They hurried off to school. They didn't even bother asking Papa if he had really told all the Bears to stop buying Grizzly goods. They just wanted to get away from the problems of the grown-up world. They were happy to get to the schoolyard and wait in peace and quiet for the morning bell.

At least, that is what they hoped to do. But after a few minutes in the schoolyard, they could tell that something was wrong.

First there was a nasty spat between Too-Tall Grizzly and Queenie McBear. And to think that just yesterday they had been strolling around arm in arm!

After that, loud arguments started all over the schoolyard. "Stupid Grizzlys!" shouted groups of Bears, "Double-stupid Bears!" shouted groups of Grizzlys. Soon the name-calling turned to kicking and punching. Teacher Bob had his hands full breaking up one fight after another.

The fighting was getting worse and worse when all of a sudden, it stopped. All eyes turned toward the gate. Squire Grizzly's chauffeur-driven limo was coming to a stop. The door opened. Out stepped a girl cub. She was wearing black velvet pants, a lavender top, and gold earrings. She was very pretty.

Suddenly all the cubs were talking at once.

"That's Squire Grizzly's niece, Bonnie Brown."

"Hey, she's *cute!*"

"Her family is living in Squire Grizzly's mansion."

"I think I've seen her before."

"Of course you have. On TV. In commercials. She's a model."

"WOW!"

Bonnie Brown made her way across the schoolyard. The boy cubs couldn't take their eyes off her.

As Brother Bear watched her, a funny feeling started in his scalp. It ran along his spine, then all the way down to the tips of his toes. Sister was about to ask him what he thought of the new girl in town. But one look at his love-struck face gave her the answer.

"Hey," she said. She snapped her fingers to wake him up. "Do you want me to pull out the arrow?"

"Arrow? What arrow?"

"Cupid's arrow. It's stuck deep in your heart."

"Aw, cut it out," Brother mumbled. He walked away and sneaked one last look at Bonnie Brown.

Teacher Bob introduced Bonnie to the class. Loud whistles and a lot of whispering filled the classroom. Teacher Bob made the class quiet down. Then he showed Bonnie to her seat. It was just across the aisle from where Brother Bear sat.

Brother couldn't help it. He had to sneak another look at the gorgeous new girl. His heart pounded so loud he thought the whole class could hear.

"All right, cubs," said Teacher Bob. "Who can give us the first answer to last night's math homework? Brother Bear?"

Brother didn't move. He was still staring at Bonnie out of the corner of his eye.

"Brother Bear? Are you with us?" asked Teacher Bob.

But still there was no answer. Cousin Freddy was sitting behind Brother. He leaned forward and poked Brother in the ribs with the eraser of his pencil. That woke Brother up. There was Teacher Bob, gazing down at him with his arms folded across his chest.

"Er . . . huh? What?" asked Brother.

"Never mind, Brother. But you had better pay attention next time. Anyone hear my question?"

Babs Bruno waved her hand and was called on. "The answer is forty-two," she said.

"Very good, Babs," said Teacher Bob. "And what formula did you use to get that answer?"

"Length times width, of course," said Babs.

"And length times width is the formula for the area of what?" asked Teacher Bob. "How about a second chance, Brother?"

Brother's eyes had drifted back to

Bonnie Brown. But he heard the question. "A heart," he said.

The whole class laughed wildly. Babs looked back at Brother and stuck out her tongue. Teacher Bob tried to quiet everyone down.

Still, Brother sneaked another look at Bonnie Brown. His heart skipped a beat. Bonnie had turned, and she was smiling at him! It wasn't a mocking smile. It was a friendly, kind, sweet smile.

With his ears burning and his collar steaming, Brother broke out into a full-strength tomato-red blush.

Chapter 4
Bonnie to the Rescue?

Brother was waiting for his turn at bat in the morning recess fistball game. Suddenly he noticed that Babs and her two friends were watching from the sidelines.

"First time I've seen Babs watching a fistball game," Brother said to Cousin Freddy. "Why do you think she's here?"

"Stop worrying," said Freddy. "You know she has a crush on you. She probably just wants to moon at you while you get a hit."

But Freddy was wrong. As Brother stepped up to bat, Babs and her friends started shouting at the top of their lungs, "Brother's in love! Brother's in love! . . ."

Brother turned bright red and missed the ball.

Babs and her friends danced around the schoolyard, singing, "Brother's got a girlfriend! Brother's got a girlfriend!"

"Boy," said Freddy. "You're in big trouble."

BROTHER'S IN LOVE! BROTHER'S IN LOVE!

Brother didn't answer him. He ducked behind a bush. Then he ran through a torn spot in the schoolyard fence and walked through the woods to an old rock pile. He sometimes went there to think things over. Brother sat slumped among the rocks.

He stayed there until he knew recess was almost over. Still he didn't budge. Brother was about to play hooky for the first time in his life.

"Brother? Are you there?"

It was a girl's voice. It came from behind the rock pile. The girl stepped forward. It was Bonnie. Brother couldn't believe it!

"B-Bonnie?" he said with a gulp. "What are you doing here?"

Bonnie sat down in front of him. "I saw the whole thing," she said. "I watched where you went and I followed you." When Brother didn't answer, she added, "I feel bad about what happened."

"Why should *you* feel bad?" Brother asked.

"I just do."

"But it's not your fault that you're so . . . cute."

Bonnie smiled. "Do you really think I'm cute?"

Brother looked off into the woods. "Please, let's not talk about stuff like that."

"Look," said Bonnie. "It doesn't help to hide from things. Listen to me. They're teasing you because they know they can get to you. Be cool. Act as if you don't care. Top them!"

"But how?" asked Brother.

"Well, they all say you have a girlfriend. So why not *have* a girlfriend?"

"But who?" asked Brother.

"What about me?" said Bonnie.

Brother felt his ears getting bright red again. He tried to catch his breath. "But . . ." he said.

"Well, I'm a girl, aren't I?" Bonnie asked.

Brother shuffled his feet.

"And we're becoming friends, aren't we?" said Bonnie.

Brother swallowed deeply.

"So come on. We'll go back there holding hands. Everyone will see us. Don't be nervous, Brother. I'm just trying to help you out—as a friend. Besides . . ." Bonnie leaned closer. "I think you're cute, too." She kissed him on the cheek.

Brother turned an even brighter shade of red.

Bonnie sat back and sighed. "But we're going to have to do something about that blushing," she said.

Chapter 5
A Friendship Torn Apart

Brother and Bonnie went back to school holding hands. It didn't stop the teasing. But it made Brother feel much better. Now he had someone on—and at—his side. And such a cute someone! When Bonnie asked him to walk home from school with her, his answer was yes.

"Thanks for coming to get me in the woods," Brother said as they strolled along. "If I had had to face all that teasing alone, I might have played hooky instead. I hope I can help you out, too, sometime."

"You can help right now," said Bonnie. "You can tell me more about this spring play that's coming up. What kinds of plays does the drama club put on?"

"Oh, the usual," said Brother. "*Robin Hood and His Merry Bears*, *Grizzlystiltskin and the Straw of Gold*, *King Arthur and the Bears of the Round Table*—that sort of thing."

"It sounds like fun," said Bonnie. "I'm glad I came to Bear Country in time to try out. You know, I do some modeling—and a little acting, too. I hope you're going to try out, too. It would be great if we could both be in the play!"

Brother felt a lump in his throat. He could hardly speak. He just swallowed hard and nodded.

Soon they came to Squire Grizzly's mansion. Brother felt very small as he looked up at the huge building.

"Have you ever been inside?" asked Bonnie.

"Once, when I was a tiny cub," he said. "I went along when my dad delivered some furniture he'd made for the Squire. But I really don't remember much."

"It's quite a place," said Bonnie. "Come on in."

"You sure it's okay?" asked Brother.

"Of course!" said Bonnie. "I live here. And you're my guest!"

Brother and Bonnie walked up the long path to the front porch with the big white pillars. Bonnie rang the doorbell.

A servant opened the heavy oak door. "Good afternoon, Miss Brown," he said, and bowed. Then he saw Brother and broke into a smile. "My goodness," he said. "Could this be Master Brother Bear? Why, I haven't seen you since you were a little cub!" But suddenly he looked worried. "Uh . . . maybe I should . . . tell the Squire you're here."

"You don't need to tell the Squire we're here," said Bonnie. "I just want to show Brother around."

"Well, yes . . . I guess so . . . for a few minutes," said the servant. He stepped back so the two could enter.

The entrance hall was two stories high! A large spiral staircase wound down from the second floor to the first. Large paintings of past squires covered the walls. At the foot of the stairs was a shiny suit of armor. With sword in hand, it seemed to be guarding the mansion.

"Gosh!" said Brother. "What a neat house!"

"Come on," said Bonnie. "I think my parents are in the sitting room. I'd like you to meet them."

Just then someone appeared at the top of the stairs. It was Squire Grizzly. Brother didn't remember him from that first visit, but he had seen so many pictures of him over the years in the *Beartown Gazette* that he knew who he was. The Squire had great side whiskers. He was wearing riding clothes

and carrying a leather riding crop.

"Hello, Bonnie," he called out in a friendly voice.

"Hi, Uncle," said Bonnie.

He began walking down the stairs. "Who is that with you?" he asked.

"It's Brother Bear," said Bonnie.

"What?!" bellowed the Squire. He raised his monocle and looked more closely. "How dare you bring that . . . that . . . that *Bear* into my home!"

"But, Uncle—" said Bonnie.

Brother felt his heart rise to his throat. He stumbled backward toward the door.

"Called me a milk poisoner, his father did!" roared the Squire. He continued down the stairs and waved his riding crop. "Now get out of here—this second!"

"Uncle!" cried Bonnie. "He's my friend! You can't throw him out!"

But Brother had already run out the door.

"And stay away from my niece!" boomed the Squire.

"It's the old feud!" Brother thought. He couldn't believe that this old grown-up fight

was happening again right here—NOW—
and to HIM!

He ran down the long path to the front
gate. Suddenly Bonnie called after him. She
was leaning from a balcony and waving.

"Brother!" she cried. "Don't go!"

Brother walked back toward the balcony.
"I . . . can't stay where I'm not welcome!"
he called.

"Then take this with you!" Bonnie
begged. She reached out and plucked a
large white flower from a vine. Then she
tossed it to Brother.

"See you in school tomorrow!" she said.

Chapter 6
A Fight Breaks Out

Mama Bear was fixing dinner when she heard Sister come down the stairs humming. "Sister," she called, "is that brother of yours home from softball yet? I have a phone message for him."

Sister came into the kitchen wearing a sly smile. "He didn't really play softball today," she said. "He's been up in his room all afternoon gazing at a flower. He's in *love.*"

Sister went on to tell Mama all about Bonnie and what had happened at Squire Grizzly's mansion.

"Oh, my goodness," said Mama. "Where did you learn all this?"

"Everybody at school knows about Brother and Bonnie. And Brother's so mad about what the Squire did that he spilled the whole story to me. Bonnie's really mad, too, he says. All they are is friends. They just met today. But now that the Squire has ordered them to stay away from each other, I think they want to go *steady.*"

"Go steady?" said Mama. "Why, just yesterday Brother was moaning about all the

romance 'mush' that's going on."

"You haven't seen Bonnie," said Sister. She grinned. "It was 'mush' at first sight."

She turned to Papa, who had come in the door a few minutes before. He looked as if he were about to explode.

"What's the matter, Papa?" said Sister.

Papa had been listening to the story of Brother and Bonnie. "What's the MATTER?" he said. He raised his voice again. "I'll tell you what's the matter!

Brother's got no business spending time with a member of that no-good, high-hat Grizzly clan! And he *would* have to pick Squire Grizzly's niece! I don't care how sweet he is on this Bonnie. It's just cub love, a silly little crush—!"

"Hold it," said Mama. "I think this feud business has gone too far! Didn't you make a big enough fool of yourself yesterday running out of gas miles from nowhere? Not to mention the terrible example you're setting for the cubs. As for me, I'm glad Brother is starting to get over his shyness toward girls."

"Shyness!" bellowed Papa. "I just can't believe my ears! Here I am trying to protect the honor of the family—of the great Bear clan—and you say you're worried about SHYNESS!?"

Just then Brother walked into the kitchen frowning. "Hey, what's all the yelling about?" he asked.

But before anyone could answer, much louder sounds came from outside the tree house. There was angry shouting and the rumbling of a large machine. And above everything, the wailing of a police siren, growing louder and closer.

The Bears hurried outside to see what was going on. There was a fight in the clover meadow! Farmer Ben was using a bulldozer to knock down Squire Grizzly's fence. The Squire had climbed onto the bulldozer and was hitting Ben with his riding crop. At the same time, Mrs. Ben was trying to poke the

Squire with a hoe handle. And Lady Grizzly, all dressed up for afternoon tea, was shaking her parasol at Mrs. Ben.

"Take that, you no-good Bear bum!" cried Squire Grizzly.

"Why, you rotten Grizzly milk spoiler!" shouted Ben.

It was quite a scene. Farmer Ben's cows even stopped eating the onion grass to watch the action.

"Hang in there, Ben! I'm coming!" cried Papa. But Mama stopped him in his tracks. Chief Bruno and Officer Marguerite had just arrived.

"Better let the chief handle this, dear," Mama said.

The Bears stood in the sweet-smelling clover and watched Chief Bruno and Officer Marguerite break up the fight. Finally, the Grizzlys stalked off to their mansion, and the Bens stalked off to their farmhouse.

"This feud is getting scary," Mama said to the chief. "I'm worried."

"YOU'RE worried," said Chief Bruno. He wiped his forehead with the back of his hand. "This is our sixth feud call today!"

Brother and Sister looked at each other and shook their heads.

Chapter 7
Choosing a Play

News of the "Clover Meadow Melee," as Bear Country historians later called it, spread faster than onion grass in a meadow. Many hoped that it would make the warring clans see how silly they were being. But that is not what happened. Instead, things got worse.

Minor traffic jams turned into shouting matches. Neighbors who had been friendly suddenly wouldn't talk to one another.

GRIZZLY CLAN
MEMBERS
NOT WELCOME

Someone even heard that a couple of elderly bears at the Bear Country Senior Citizens' Home were fighting in their wheelchairs.

Some of the kindest bears became mean and nasty. Biff Bruin put a big cardboard sign in the window of his pharmacy. It said *Grizzly Clan Members Not Welcome*.

And then there was Ralph Ripoff, who was always looking for ways to make some fast money. This time he made a bundle going door-to-door selling "feud buttons." To the Grizzlys, he sold his "Grizzly Pride!" buttons. To the Bears, he sold his "Bears Stand Tall!" buttons.

In the meantime, Teacher Bob's Drama Club met at the Bear Country Playhouse to decide on a spring play. "Does anyone have any suggestions?" asked Teacher Bob.

"How about *King Arthur and the Bears of the Round Table?*" asked Cousin Freddy.

"*Snow White and the Seven Cubs!*" shouted Babs Bruno.

"*Robin Hood and His Merry Bears!*" said Too-Tall Grizzly. He pretended to shoot an arrow from a make-believe bow. Everyone knew who he thought should play Robin Hood.

"Those are all good plays," said Teacher Bob, "but I have a better idea. Isn't there something very troubling going on in Bear Country right now? What do you cubs think about what is going on?"

"Do you mean the feud?" asked Brother. He looked at Bonnie Brown, who was sitting right next to him. She nodded.

"Yes, exactly," said Teacher Bob.

The cubs all said that they didn't like the feud. But they didn't see what it had to do with the spring play.

So Teacher Bob held up a large book called *The Plays of William Shakesbeare.* "Tell me, what do you cubs know about Shakesbeare?" he asked.

Queenie McBear stood up. "I know that he's for grownups. And that means he must be really boring," she said.

The class broke out in giggles. Teacher Bob raised a hand to stop the laughter. "'Boring,' you say?" Then he grabbed a piece of chalk and wrote *Romeo and Juliet* on the blackboard. "Does anyone know what this play is about?" he asked.

No one answered.

"Well," he said, "it's about two young lovers. Now does that sound *boring?*"

"No way!" said Babs Bruno from the back of the room. "That sounds like two cubs we know!"

Loud hoots, hollers, and laughs filled the room. Everyone looked over at Brother and Bonnie.

"Hey, look at him blush!" shouted Queenie.

That made Brother's face turn beet red.

Too-Tall started to kiss the back of his hand with sloppy, loud smacking noises. "I love you! I love you!" he moaned.

Brother stood up and shook his fist at Too-Tall. "You had better shut up about Bonnie and me!" he yelled.

"Oh, yeah? And what if I don't?" Too-Tall yelled back.

"Then I'll knock you right on your big tin can!" said Brother.

Brother started to move toward the bigger cub, but Teacher Bob stepped between them. "You two sit down right now and pay attention!" he said. Brother and Too-Tall did as they were told. Teacher Bob wrote on the blackboard: "sword fights, poison, death!" The cubs' eyes opened wide. "All of these things happen in *Romeo and Juliet*," he said, "because of a feud between

two clans—the Capulet family and the Montague family."

The cubs were all very quiet for a moment.

Then Sister Bear cried, "A feud! A feud between two clans! That sounds just like what is going in Bear Country!"

"Right!" said Teacher Bob. "Now, all the grownups will be coming to the spring play. Maybe if we do a good job of putting on this play, we can show them just what could happen if they keep fighting."

Every cub in the room voted for *Romeo and Juliet* for the spring play.

Chapter 8

The Blushing Champion
of Bear Country

Tryouts for the part of Juliet were held first. When Bonnie Brown got the part, Brother knew he had to try out for Romeo. He was embarrassed at the thought of playing Romeo while Bonnie played Juliet. But the thought of anyone else playing Romeo was even worse. So he tried out.

Even though Brother's reading for the part was a little shy and clumsy, Teacher Bob gave Brother the part. He knew that everyone in the class wanted Brother to play Romeo, since Bonnie was playing Juliet.

One by one, the other parts were filled. Too-Tall Grizzly and Queenie McBear got the parts of Lord and Lady Capulet, Juliet's parents. Frank Furry and Lizzy Bruin got the parts of Montague and Lady Montague, Romeo's parents. Babs Bruno was to play Juliet's nursemaid. Barry Bruin would play a character named Mercutio.

Cousin Freddy was happy as both stage manager and set designer. He even built some of the sets by himself. He was especially proud of the wooden balcony he built for the famous scene where Juliet looks down from the balcony at Romeo while he looks up at her and tells her he loves her.

The first rehearsal went well—until the famous balcony scene. When Bonnie set foot on the balcony—CRUNCH—it fell apart!

"Romeo! Romeo!" Bonnie yelled as she came crashing down. But luckily, she fell straight into Brother's arms! She didn't even have a scratch! All the members of the cast clapped wildly for Brother, who turned beet red and gently lowered Bonnie to the floor.

At first, Freddy couldn't figure out what had gone wrong. "Let's see, now," he said. He scratched his head and picked up a few

pieces of the broken balcony. "I believe that the gravitational forces pulling Bonnie down were greater than the structural supports holding the balcony up, and . . ."

Freddy finally figured it all out, and the scenery crew worked late into the night making repairs. Finally, Brother and Bonnie were able to rehearse the balcony scene without any surprises.

Bonnie played Juliet beautifully. Brother had some trouble at first but then quickly got the hang of acting. It helped him to be so crazy about the leading lady. In fact, ever since her uncle and his father had said they couldn't see each other, Brother's crush had gotten even stronger. He was able to put all his true feelings into the role of Romeo.

There was only one problem. It was a big one. No matter how many times Brother rehearsed the kissing scene with Bonnie, he couldn't stop himself from blushing.

Brother's blushing became such a problem that Teacher Bob started to worry that the audience would laugh. If that happened, *Romeo and Juliet* would no longer be a tragedy. It would become a comedy. And the whole point would be lost. The feuding grownups wouldn't learn their lesson.

A few days before opening night, Bonnie came up with a plan to stop Brother's blushing. "Meet me after school at the old rock pile in the woods," she whispered to Brother after rehearsal.

Bonnie was waiting for Brother as he came through the woods. "What's up?" he asked.

"We're going to break you of your blushing habit," said Bonnie.

"Okay, but how?" asked Brother.

"It's simple. We'll just keep kissing until you get used to it and stop blushing!" said Bonnie.

"Gee, I don't know about that, Bonnie. I mean, I've never kissed a girl before . . . I mean, in real life," said Brother.

"Then it's time to start," said Bonnie.

"But I don't know about our meeting here like this . . . in the woods . . . to practice . . . uh . . . *kissing*," said Brother.

"Good grief! You're blushing already!" said Bonnie. "Besides, we're not practicing kissing, really. We're rehearsing for a very important play. Opening night is only two days away. If you don't learn to stop blushing when we kiss, the whole play will be a big joke. And if that happens, the stupid grown-up feud will go on and on and get worse and worse. And we won't be able to be friends anymore. It will be hard for any Bears and Grizzlys to be friends anymore! What do you think of that, Brother Bear?"

She looked Brother right in the eye. "Well?" she said with her hands on her hips. "What are we going to do about it?"

"I guess we're going to kiss," said Brother.

They kissed.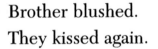

Brother blushed.
They kissed again.

Brother blushed again.

They kissed again and again and again.

Brother blushed again and again and again.

Bonnie sighed. "It just isn't working," she said. But she wouldn't give up. "There must be a way." She thought for a second. "Wait!" she cried. "I have an idea!"

Brother didn't know what to say. He didn't have any ideas. He felt as if his brain had turned to mush from so much kissing. "What's your idea?" he asked.

"Remember how hard you blushed at that first Drama Club meeting? When the whole club ganged up on us?" asked Bonnie.

"So what else is new?" said Brother.

"Think back," said Bonnie. "When Too-Tall came on a little bit stronger, you stopped blushing."

"Yeah," said Brother. "The big creep got me so mad that I forgot all about being embarrassed."

"That's it!" said Bonnie. "Every time we kiss, just think about knocking that big

creep on his tin can! Now think hard—"

Brother and Bonnie held their breath and kissed once again. It worked! Brother thought about being angry at Too-Tall, and he didn't blush one bit!

"You see?" said Bonnie. "It's all a question of mind over matter."

"Don't you mean mind over mush?" said Brother, grinning. He and Bonnie had a good laugh. Then they hurried back to school to tell Teacher Bob that the play was saved.

Chapter 9
What Light Through Yonder Window Breaks?

It was the night of the spring play! The cast waited nervously backstage while the audience took their seats.

Most of the Grizzlys came into the theater through one door and most of the

Bears through another. Farmer Ben and Squire Grizzly got into a snarling spat even before they had reached their seats.

Luckily, Chief Bruno had provided extra officers. This stopped any real trouble from breaking out. Finally, the whole audience was seated.

When the curtain rose, everyone had a big surprise. Cousin Freddy was still onstage touching up the scenery! And he had no idea that the curtain had risen. But suddenly he turned around. There was the whole audience, staring at him! Freddy was so shocked that all he could do was look for

his parents in the crowd and say, "Hi, Mom . . . Hi, Dad!" Then he waved and ran quickly off the stage. The audience broke into laughter. Luckily, that took away some of the tense feeling in the room. The play was ready to begin.

The cubs did a wonderful job. The audience seemed to be under a spell. They barely moved in their seats. There were cries of shock and horror as the Capulets and Montagues fought with one another for no good reason. There were shrieks and gasps when the brave Mercutio was killed in a sword fight. And there were sighs of happiness when Romeo and Juliet met secretly.

During the balcony scene, Papa Bear, the Bens, and Squire and Lady Grizzly all had huge lumps in their throats. So did Cousin Freddy—but for a very different reason!

Even the kissing scene between Brother and Bonnie went smoothly. Teacher Bob had been afraid that that scene would make Papa Bear and Squire Grizzly leap up onstage to pull the two lovers apart. But that did not happen. And Brother didn't blush!

By the end of the play, the audience was in a state of shock. There were Romeo and Juliet, dying in each other's arms. And it was all because of a feud between their families. The audience was silent and still.

The curtain came down and the lights came up.

All through the audience, Grizzly clan members and Bear clan members turned to one another and smiled. Many reached out and shook hands warmly. Then they began to clap.

Soon the applause became so loud that the curtain rose once again.

The cast took another bow.

The grownups of Bear Country were so thankful. They clapped for so long that the cubs took *ten* curtain calls!

Then Teacher Bob was called up onstage to take a bow.

Chapter 10
The Party

After the play, Queenie McBear held a cast party at her house. There was lots of music and food.

Everyone was in a good mood for two reasons. They knew they had done a fine acting job. And they knew that their parents had ended the old feud of Bear Country.

Brother Bear and Bonnie were drinking sodas and talking about the play when Queenie rushed over to them. She had a big smile on her face. "Congratulations, you two!" she cried.

"Thanks, Queenie," said Brother.

"Yeah," said Bonnie. "You were great, too."

"Oh, I didn't mean your acting," said Queenie with a wink.

"No?" said Brother. "Then what *did* you mean?"

"Now that the feud between the clans is over, you two are free—free to go steady! See you later, lovers!"

Queenie dashed off. Brother and Bonnie looked at each other in surprise.

"She's right, you know," said Bonnie. She looked Brother straight in the eye.

Brother felt a little confused. Bonnie was as cute as ever—that was for sure. But something was bothering him. It had been great being in the play and getting rid of the feud. And he knew that Bonnie was a terrific cub. He *really* liked her. But he wasn't so sure about this "going steady."

It seemed strange to Brother that when he wasn't allowed to see Bonnie, she was all

he could think of. It had been exciting and daring to see her. But now that they were allowed to see each other, well . . . it just wasn't the same. It felt sort of dumb. He remembered something Gran had once said about forbidden fruit tasting the sweetest. He couldn't figure out what she was talking about at the time, but now he understood.

"I think I know what you are thinking, Brother," said Bonnie suddenly.

"Huh?" said Brother. He was thinking so deeply that he had forgotten Bonnie was there.

"You're thinking you're not so sure about going steady," said Bonnie.

Brother felt he should tell Bonnie she was wrong. But before he could, Bonnie grinned and said, "It's okay, Brother. I sort of feel the same way."

"You *do?*" said Brother. "Hey, terrific!" He couldn't believe how things were working out. He wouldn't have to miss the season's soccer and softball games?

"Positively," she said. "I need a friend a lot more than I need a boyfriend."

"And I need a friend a lot more than I need a girlfriend," said Brother.

The two smiled at each other. Brother breathed a sigh of relief.

Just then Queenie said it was time for a kissing game—post office. "This game is in honor of Bear Country's great lovers, Brother Bear and Bonnie Brown," she said with a big smile.

"What do we do now?" asked Brother. "Everyone thinks we're great lovers. How can we let them down?"

"I'll take care of that," said Bonnie. "Just leave it to me."

One by one, the girls took turns inviting their favorite boys into the "mail room," which was really the McBear laundry room. At last it was Bonnie's turn.

Brother took a deep breath.

"I have a bunch of special deliveries," said Bonnie, "for . . . Brother Bear!" The other cubs hooted and hollered and whistled. Frowning, Brother followed Bonnie into the "mail room." He closed the door behind them.

It was dark inside, but a little light crept in around the door. Outside, the gang was yelling, "Hey, wherefore art thou, Romeo?" and "Okay, guys, let's get it on! Ready! Pucker up! Smacko!"

"So what are we going to do, Bonnie?" asked Brother. "I'm all kissed out from the play."

"Me too," said Bonnie with a giggle. "But

here's what we'll do. You moan and groan,
and I'll take care of the 'special deliveries.'
We'll send the cubs home happy."

Then Bonnie pressed her lips to the back
of her hand and made loud smacking noises.
Brother moaned as if he were having a great
time. After being silent for a few seconds,
they finally came out of the laundry room.
The other cubs cheered and howled and
clapped wildly.

With a big smile, Brother put an arm around Bonnie's shoulder and said, "Nothing to it, gang. Nothing to it."

And he didn't even blush.

Stan and Jan Berenstain began writing and illustrating books for children in the early 1960s, when their two young sons were beginning to read. That marked the start of the best-selling Berenstain Bears series. Now, with more than 95 books in print, videos, television shows, and even a Berenstain Bears theme park, it's hard to tell where the Bears end and the Berenstains begin!

Stan and Jan make their home in Bucks County, Pennsylvania, and plan on writing and illustrating many more books for children, especially for their four grandchildren, who keep them well in touch with the kids of today.